500

COTTAGES

DOUGLAS KEISTER

The Taunton Press

DEDICATED TO THE COTTAGE HOMEOWNERS
WHO PRESERVE THE PAST TO BETTER THE FUTURE.

The Taunton Press

The Taunton Press, Inc.
63 South Main Street, PO Box 5506
Newtown, CT 06470-5506
e-mail: tp@taunton.com

Editor: Pam Hoenig
Jacket/Cover design: Chika Azuma
Interior design: Chika Azuma
Layout: Cathy Cassidy
Photographer: Douglas Keister

Library of Congress Cataloging-in-Publication Data

Keister, Douglas.
 500 cottages / Douglas Keister.
 p. cm.
 ISBN-13: 978-1-56158-843-5
 ISBN-10: 1-56158-843-1
 1. Cottages--United States--Pictorial works. 2. Architecture--United States--
20th century--Pictorial works. I. Title: Five hundred cottages. II. Title.
 NA7208.K45 2006
 728'.370973--dc22

 2006006818

 Printed in China
 10 9 8 7 6 5 4 3 2 1

The following manufacturers/names appearing in *500 Cottages* are trademarks: Formica®

CONTENTS

INTRODUCTION

2

STORYBOOK COTTAGES

4

CASITAS

122

BUNGALETTES

176

PERIOD REVIVAL COTTAGES

246

VICTORIAN COTTAGES

290

ECLECTIC COTTAGES

414

Scholars tell us that cottages are small, romantic dwellings that are usually scaled down and less formal counterparts of larger, more ostentatious residences. Thus, looming, gingerbread-festooned Victorians become Queen Anne cottages, Carpenter Gothic gems, and Italianate mini-palaces. Rambling Spanish-style mansions become casitas; Arts and Crafts extravaganzas are compressed into bungalows; and European castles become charming storybook style cottages. The allure of the more relaxed cottage lifestyle is so strong that even 19th-century titans of industry built 70-room "cottages" that lined the streets of fashionable Newport, Rhode Island. To be sure, their Gilded Age mega-cottages were hardly the simple romantic homes most think of when we dream of these tidy houses, but strictly speak-

ing, the summer cottages of the Vanderbilts and Astors were scaled down and less formal interpretations of their over-the-top urban mansions.

I grew up in a cottage. My boyhood home sits on a quiet tree-lined street in Lincoln, Nebraska. The construction and architecture of my family's postwar cottage was absolutely unremarkable, although if one squinted just right, the house had the vague look of a Cape Cod cottage. For three young boys it was more like a playhouse, far different than our relatives' larger, ranch-style homes with their off-limits-for-kids areas. No areas of our home were off limits; we used every square foot with abandon. And that's what makes a cottage so wonderful. It's a home that gets used. It's family, it's mom and apple pie—it's home.

—Douglas Keister, Chico, California

STORYBOOK COTTAGES

CHARLEVOIX, MICHIGAN 13

40　CHARLEVOIX, MICHIGAN

52 OAKLAND, CALIFORNIA

70 CHARLEVOIX, MICHIGAN

88 ALBANY, CALIFORNIA

CASITAS

134 SAN DIEGO, CALIFORNIA

BUNGALETTES

PACIFIC GROVE, CALIFORNIA

188 PASADENA, CALIFORNIA

190 PASADENA, CALIFORNIA

208 SAN DIEGO, CALIFORNIA

212 NASHVILLE, TENNESSEE

214 KISSIMMEE, FLORIDA

216 SAN JOSE, CALIFORNIA

PERIOD REVIVAL COTTAGES

258 BELLINGHAM, WASHINGTON

ALAMEDA, CALIFORNIA

VICTORIAN COTTAGES

302 SHARTLESVILLE, PENNSYLVANIA

308 PACIFIC GROVE, CALIFORNIA

320 ASPEN, COLORADO

334　San Francisco, California

386 SAN JOSE, CALIFORNIA

412 HEALDSBURG, CALIFORNIA

ECLECTIC COTTAGES

ANYA'S HOUSE COTTAGE | Hana, Maui, Hawaii

416 MODERN-STYLE COTTAGE | SAN DIEGO, CALIFORNIA

ENGLISH-STYLE COTTAGE | CHICO, CALIFORNIA 417

420 ENGLISH-STYLE COTTAGE | San Diego, California

ENGLISH-STYLE COTTAGE | St. Paul, Minnesota 423

PLANTATION-STYLE COTTAGE | Lahaina, Maui, Hawaii

ENGLISH-STYLE COTTAGE | CHICO, CALIFORNIA

434 BAY OF FUNDY, NOVA SCOTIA, CANADA

HAMOA BEACH COTTAGE | Hana, Maui, Hawaii

ENGLISH-STYLE COTTAGE | OAKLAND, CALIFORNIA 437

440 SLAVE COTTAGE | LAURA PLANTATION, LOUISIANA

ENGLISH-STYLE COTTAGE | SAN DIEGO, CALIFORNIA 441

442 JAPANESE PLANTATION COTTAGE | Honolulu, Hawaii

ENGLISH-STYLE COTTAGE | San Francisco, California 443

446 ST. PAUL, MINNESOTA

PLANTATION-STYLE COTTAGE | LAHAINA, MAUI, HAWAII

ORIENTAL-STYLE COTTAGE | HONOLULU, HAWAII 449

ENGLISH-STYLE COTTAGE | St. Paul, Minnesota

TEEPEE COTTAGE | WORKMAN TEMPLE HOMESTEAD INDUSTRY, CITY OF INDUSTRY, CALIFORNIA

ALOHA BALI COTTAGE | OLINDA, MAUI, HAWAII

ENGLISH-STYLE COTTAGE | MINNEAPOLIS, MINNESOTA

CREOLE COTTAGE | New Orleans, Louisiana 455

456 PASADENA, CALIFORNIA

NEUTRA COTTAGE | SAN DIEGO, CALIFORNIA 457

SHOTGUN COTTAGE | NEW ORLEANS, LOUISIANA

ENGLISH-STYLE COTTAGE | MINNEAPOLIS, MINNESOTA

PACIFIC GROVE, CALIFORNIA 461

462 ENGLISH-STYLE COTTAGE | SAN DIEGO, CALIFORNIA

464 ENGLISH-STYLE COTTAGE | DEL MAR, CALIFORNIA

HOTEL HANA-MAUI COTTAGE | Hana, Maui, Hawaii 467

KOREAN-STYLE COTTAGE | HONOLULU, HAWAII 469

WILD GINGER FALLS COTTAGE | Makawao, Maui, Hawaii

SHOTGUN COTTAGE | New Orleans, Louisiana 475

PLANTATION-STYLE COTTAGE | Honolulu, Hawaii

ENGLISH-STYLE COTTAGE | MINNEAPOLIS, MINNESOTA 477

478 PORTUGUESE-STYLE COTTAGE | Maui, Hawaii

PLANTATION-STYLE COTTAGE | Lahaina, Maui, Hawaii

SHOTGUN COTTAGE | ALGIERS, LOUISIANA

ORIENTAL-STYLE COTTAGE | HONOLULU, HAWAII 487

490　MODERN-STYLE COTTAGE | SAN DIEGO, CALIFORNIA

ENGLISH-STYLE COTTAGE | DEL MAR, CALIFORNIA 491

PLANTATION-STYLE COTTAGE | OLINDA, MAUI, HAWAII

MODERN-STYLE COTTAGE | SAN DIEGO, CALIFORNIA 493

PLANTATION-STYLE COTTAGE | LAHAINA, MAUI, HAWAII

SHOTGUN COTTAGE | New Orleans, Louisiana 495

496 ENGLISH-STYLE COTTAGE | St. Paul, Minnesota

ENGLISH-STYLE COTTAGE | SAN DIEGO, CALIFORNIA 497

PLANTATION-STYLE COTTAGE | Lahaina, Maui, Hawaii

ST. PAUL, MINNESOTA 503

ASHEVILLE, NORTH CAROLINA 505

SHOTGUN COTTAGE | New Orleans, Louisiana

508 CHICO, CALIFORNIA

PLANTATION-STYLE COTTAGE | Lahaina, Maui, Hawaii 509

DOUGLAS KEISTER IS AMERICA'S MOST NOTED PHOTOGRAPHER OF HISTORIC RESIDENTIAL ARCHITECTURE. HIS 31 BOOKS INCLUDE 12 BOOKS ON BUNGALOWS, BOOKS ON COTTAGES, STORYBOOK-STYLE HOMES, SPANISH HOMES, AND CEMETERIES, AS WELL AS A CHILDREN'S BOOK AND TWO ART BOOKS. HE ALSO WRITES AND ILLUSTRATES MAGAZINE ARTICLES FOR A VARIETY OF PUBLICATIONS. FIND HIM ON THE WEB AT WWW.KEISTERPHOTO.COM. HE LIVES IN CHICO, CALIFORNIA, WITH HIS WIFE, SANDY.